THE MEDIOCRE TEACHER PROJECT

Keys to overcoming teacher burnout in and outside the classroom

Seven educators share their enduring story of escaping the "mediocrity trap" and taking back control of their classroom and life

Foreword by Owen M. Griffith, M.ED.

DR. MARQUITA S. BLADES

Copyright © 2018 Dr. Marquita S. Blades

All rights reserved. No part of this publication may be reproduced, distributed, or transmitted in any form or by any means, including photocopying, recording, or other electronic or mechanical methods, without the prior written permission of the publisher, except in the case of brief quotations embodied in critical reviews and certain other noncommercial uses permitted by copyright law.

Scripture quotations taken from the Holy Bible, King James Version.

Printed in the United States of America

ISBN-13: 978-0-692-18481-3
ISBN-10: 0-692-18481-3

TABLE OF CONTENTS

Foreword v

Chapter 1: Confessions of a Mediocre Teacher 1
by Dr. Marquita S. Blades

Chapter 2: Trapped..21
by Dr. Ragan M. Brown

Chapter 3: Putting Lipstick On A Pig........................46
by Melody A. Herb

Chapter 4: Is The Classroom For Me?......................57
by Dee Harris

Chapter 5: The Jill of All Trades 70
by Minister Ranyel L. Trent

Chapter 6: The Flames of Mediocrity!......................83
by Carole Cramer-Banks

Chapter 7: While Waiting..99
by Dr. Kemi Popoola

OTHER BOOKS BY DR. MARQUITA S. BLADES

Chronicles of the Chronically Ill (#1 Bestseller)

POWARRFUL Teaching Strategies for Increasing Engagement and Maintaining Rigor in Science Courses

The Whole Truth, & Nothing But The Truth, So Help Me Teachers! (Co-Author) (Award Winning Compilation)

Lessons From My Grandmother's Lap (Co-Author)

Purchase copies at www.drmarquitablades.com/shop

FOREWORD

by Owen M. Griffith
Author of Gratitude: A Way of Teaching

I have had the tremendous pleasure of working with Dr. Marquita Blades and seeing the positive impact her work with the Mediocre Teacher Project is having on education locally and also nationally. Currently, we are experiencing a crisis in education and this book and the larger project can spearhead a new direction in education as it helps teacher reflect and focus on becoming transformational educators.

In this book, you will read inspirational stories that can help empower educators across the planet. Also, some of the strategies and advice are instantly applicable, as well as helping guide long term goals and success.

Let me share my own experience with being a "mediocre" teacher and how I was able to grow out of that trap. Teaching is a challenging endeavor. With all the demands on a teacher's time and energy, it is easy to lose the enthusiasm that brought us into the classroom. In addition, teachers have recently had new requirements added to their load, including standardized testing and dealing with the Common-Core. However, there is good news. Recent research and personal experience have shown that gratitude, a simple yet powerful tool, may be applied in your classroom to improve the culture as well as raising the student's grades and goals.

An Eager New Teacher: The Dream and the Reality-The Challenges and the Miracles

My first year teaching, I entered the classroom with idealistic dreams. I went through extra training in pedagogy that tempered those lofty goals and gave me many tools I was eager to use. I taught 7th grade science in an inner-city school and saw 120 students a day. Sadly, within a few weeks, dealing with a multitude of challenges, I quickly slipped into survival mode and questioned my decision to become a teacher. But small, and sometimes tremendous, miracles did happen that kept me moving forward.

Because I had been practicing gratitude and keeping a gratitude list, I still kept a decent attitude through all the challenges of that first year. A fellow teacher commented that even though my first year was tough and she saw me struggle, I kept the most positive attitude she had ever seen. That positive outlook did help me, but I didn't see how it could apply with the students yet.

Of all the things I have done in my life, getting through my first year of teaching was by far my most challenging undertaking. And yes, during that first year, I would reach those transcendent moments where I did connect with the student and felt the magic that happens when the classroom unites in learning.

Angel

During my first week of teaching, one day I came across one of my students, Angel, sitting in the hallway with some sheet music. I asked, "Are you a musician?" She said, "No, but I love to sing and I am learning a new song." I asked her if she would sing for me, but Angel said, "No, Mr. Griffith, I am too shy." As I walked away I said, "Someday, when you are ready, you will sing for me."

Then, a month later, Angel saw me in hallway and said, "Mr. Griffith, I am ready today." I tried to think about what she meant. Through the tornado of activity that first month, I forgot about that previous interaction. But, she pulled out the sheet music, and I remembered it all. I realized that she had been working for a month on the song and getting her courage up just for this day. I asked her if she would perform for the class, but she said, "No, I will sing just for you."

When the students all exited the classroom, she closed her eyes, and a voice came out of her that fit her name. It truly seemed like an angel had entered the classroom as she sang. I closed my eyes and enjoyed connecting with her on a different level.

As I listened, I also realized the power we have as teachers to inspire, and that when we challenge our students, they will often respond positively. In addition, she inspired me to bring my guitar into the classroom and share music with my students, integrating it into class. While she grew in her courage through this interaction, I grew in my ability to connect with my students by seeing that there are many ways to reach students outside the traditional paradigms.

As the year progressed, I kept doing the things that worked, but lack of effective classroom management was getting in the way of my lessons. This was a challenging school, and I was breaking up fights in my classroom, as well as dealing with students who had given up on life by the 7th grade. I wanted to reach all these students so much, but I could only connect from time to time with a small fraction of them.

Many nights, I would wake up at 3 AM, haunted by all the things going wrong with my teaching. This is when I would do a personal gratitude list and still find the good things happening among all the apparent problems. This kept me going through those darkest hours. Just when I thought of quitting and going back to my old career, another major miracle happened.

Robert

Robert was a tough 7th grader who didn't seem to care about school or anything else. By his own admission, he was on the brink of joining a gang and failing every subject. When I would pass out the science assignment for the day, he would say, "Mr. G., science doesn't mean anything in my life." Then, he would ceremoniously crumple up the assignment and throw it in the trash saying, "I'll take an 'F' for the day." This bothered me tremendously, and I tried different things to reach him, but didn't seem to get through.

Then after Christmas Break, one day I handed out a new assignment about the scientific method. Surprisingly, Robert looked intently at the page and said, "Will you help me with this Mr. G?" After what he said registered in my brain, I quickly went to his desk and guided him through the scientific method. On the way home that night, I found myself smiling and wondering what happened to Robert. The next thing that ran through my mind was, "Will this change last, or was it a one day anomaly?"

The next day, we delved further into the scientific method, and Robert asked more questions. Even more shocking, he started helping some of his fellow students who used to throw the papers away right along with Robert. Robert's turn around came at my darkest hour in the classroom. I don't know if I would have kept going if it hadn't been for this minor miracle.

But I realized it wasn't just a minor miracle. When a student who was thinking about joining a gang and failing every subject turned around and not only got straight A's in my science class but also got straight A's in every subject by the end of the year, helped other students in academics, and stayed out of trouble, I realized I was a small part of a major transformation. When I had one award to give at the end of the year, I gave it to Robert and felt overwhelmed with joy as he walked across the stage at the assembly to receive his award. His parents came to the ceremony and were beaming with the same joy we all shared that day.

Astonished and encouraged by this student's turn around, I asked my mentor if she had a student like this every year, and she said that she has not had any students like this in her seven years of teaching. I examined Robert's dramatic about face with his other teachers, but we could not locate that specific instance that changed him and got him on a positive track. When I asked Robert what had happened, he said, "You never gave up on me and kept trying with me, Mr. G." I was reminded of a saying from a pedagogy course that said, "All it takes to change a student's life is the appropriate adult at the appropriate time."

Even with these phenomenal students, by the end of my first year, I was exhausted and wanted to take a year off to re-examine my decision to become a teacher. I almost became part of that sad statistic that says almost half the teachers leave the profession in the first few years. But, a great opportunity was presented to teach 4th graders at a new school in a new city. This time, I had some experience and knew that I would do things differently.

Gratitude Can Change Your Classroom

To start the new year of teaching, I knew I needed to get a better classroom management program. I was paired with another teacher who had eleven years of experience and was a master teacher. As we planned for the year, she noted that I had a tremendously positive attitude and asked how I cultivated this sunny disposition. I told her that I work at it by keeping a gratitude journal. Intrigued and a bit skeptical, she said she wanted to try it.

Within a few weeks, she commented on how much it helped her. One day as we were planning for the first day of school, I had the inspiration of trying gratitude in the classroom. I realized that this could be a breakthrough. If it worked for me and others, it would work for the students. Also, this was a chance to interject some of my personality into my teaching and dramatically improve the culture of the classroom.

So, when the students arrived, we started a gratitude journal from the first day of class. That was ten years ago, and as those students are preparing for college now, many of them still keep their gratitude logs, but some have updated them to their computers or iPhone.

One parent shared with me that she was cleaning up her son's room and found something underneath his bed. Surprised, she opened the book and saw it was his gratitude journal that he had started in my class and was still updating into high school. Carefully, she returned it to his hiding place with a smile, knowing her son had taken the practice of gratitude to heart. She said she was glad her son would be practicing gratitude throughout his life, that it was an "essential" skill that would benefit him in many endeavors.

Gratitude was the missing element for me in the classroom, bringing about a positive and improving culture that only seemed to improve as the year went on. Furthermore, gratitude had a cascading effect that gave me more energy to devote to every aspect of teaching, from planning lessons to dealing with conflict between students, to keeping the students interested in school as the year dragged on.

Now, as I reflect on utilizing gratitude for ten years in my classroom, I see how practicing gratitude personally and in my classroom has empowered me to teach more effectively, to appreciate my individual students, to grow in my profession, and to enjoy life. I am able to model one of the most important lessons in life, having a positive attitude, especially about the aspects of life that challenge me.

In fact, a few years ago, I was voted teacher of the year at my school, a direct result of practicing conscious gratitude in my life, in my classroom, with my colleagues, and in my personal life. A teaching career that has gratefully passed beyond mediocrity. So, please read this book and allow it to inspire you to transform as a teacher and change the world!

"It is happening. I trust the process!"
- Dr. Marquita S. Blades

1

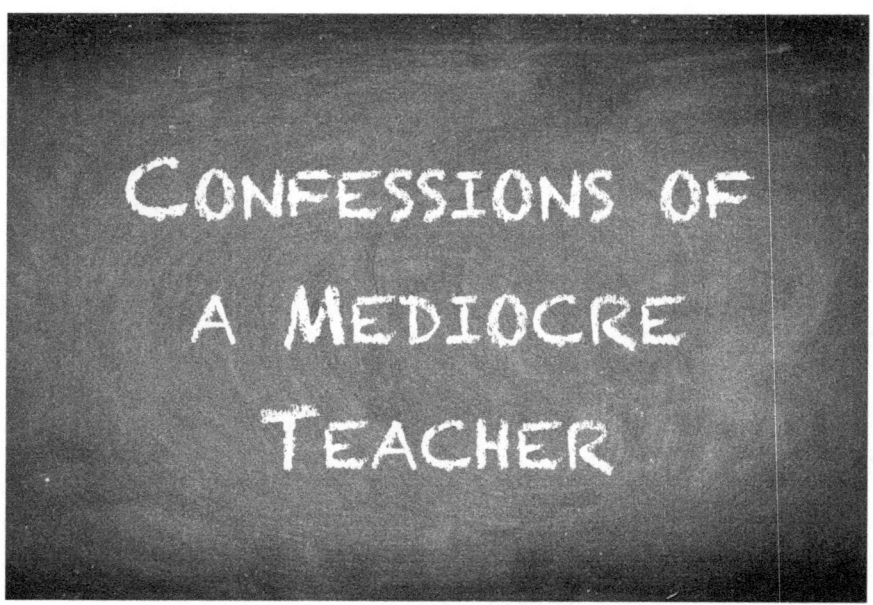

by Dr. Marquita S. Blades

At one time, teaching was my life. It was all I'd ever wanted to do. Now I'm glad I no longer have to enter a classroom on a daily basis. These are my confessions!

Confession #1: I loved teaching, but hated going to work.

If only teachers were left alone to teach, how wonderful the job would be. But we all know that's not the case. There are so many other duties that are placed upon teachers that we barely have any time to teach. Let's see... we have to attend faculty meetings, serve on committees, and make social work referrals. We have to be aware of every kid's home life and are expected to meet everyone's needs simultaneously.

Confession #2: I hated grading papers, well, most of them.

For the most part, I always had a hard time keeping up with grading papers. I had to find some strategies to assess students and provide them feedback without getting bogged down with paper grading. That came later in my career. In the earlier years, I did what teachers do. I gave assignments, collected them, would start to grade them during planning but get distracted, and the papers would pile up.

<u>Confession #3: I hated writing lesson plans.</u>

As a science teacher, it never made sense to me why I had to spend 3-4 hours per week writing about what I was going to do in science when I could have been prepping the materials to actually do the science. Now, don't get me wrong, I'm not saying I did not plan. Heck, I love to plan. I write everything down in advance and love lists. The planning part is not the issue. It's the lesson planning that gets me. Let me see if I can explain.

I have always kept a planner strictly for teaching. This is where I like to "lesson plan". Rather than using some stale template with a bunch of stuff that no one is going to even look at, I would write my standard for the week and the topics/activities for each day in my planner. I always knew what my targets were and what each class would be doing in advance. I did what worked for me.

When I went from working in a school district that did not require lesson plans to be turned in, to one where they were, it was a complete culture shock. Where was I supposed to get an extra 3-4 hours per week to get this work done? I already had a problem getting papers graded and working at home really wasn't my thing unless I had some bright idea for a project of lab that I wanted to do. Listen, most teachers have at least a little bit of a creative side. That creativity is killed when they have to fill in templates with arbitrary buzzwords that have nothing to do with real teaching and learning.

Confession #4: I think evaluations (as they are currently conducted) are pointless.

For the life of me, I can't understand how a teacher's position can be hinged upon the observations made during a 20-, at most, 30-minute visit by an administrator. Often, administrators are making observations in classrooms where subjects they are not proficient in are being taught. If they don't see everything on their checklist during this short period of time, it is possible a teacher could be labeled ineffective, although that teacher may have been stellar just five minutes before the administrator walked in.

I'm not advocating for the lack of accountability on the part of teachers. I know there are some teachers who are closing the door when the bell rings and not doing what they are supposed to do. However, those are few and far between.

Most teachers are working hard to help students learn and they are doing the best that they can. Their best work is being done when no one is looking. There is absolutely no way a 20-minute visit can indicate the full scope of an individual's talent and dedication. This is the argument that is made regarding students and testing, but I guess the same can't be said of the teachers.

Confession #5: I always wished I could pick my own students rather than having them assigned.

I want to teach who I want to teach. Sorry, but I'm not offering any apologies for this. I was in the classroom for a very long time and I know the type of students who benefit most from my style of teaching. I have some effective strategies that work well with getting any and all students engaged. I understand that you have to meet students where they are and adjust your practice to suit their needs. Yep. Got it! However, my best work is done with a particular type of student and if I were to ever teach again, that would be the only type of student I'd teach.

We all have our strengths and weaknesses. Some people are good at motivating, some are good at informing, and others are good at assisting. Some students learn best from teachers who encourage, some students learn best from teachers who tell, and other students learn best from teachers who provide one-on-one help. Why not allow teachers to work with students who can benefit most from their talents?

Every summer when I was teaching, we'd have to fill out a schedule request for the upcoming school year. Every fall, when we returned, the schedule would be completely different from what teachers had requested. I never understood why we played the game of submitted preferences that would only be ignored.

When teachers aren't excited about the work, students suffer. I'm not sure why administrators think it is cute to assign a teacher who is weak on discipline a class full of behavior problems. Taking the time to build relationships – by observing teachers more often than twice a year for 20 minutes – is a great place to start! Let teachers teach the courses they request. They'll be happier, more productive, and more effective for their students.

I get that there are restrictions with certifications and who can teach what, but then I have to argue that this is where strategic hiring comes in.

Confession #6: I'm horrible at classroom management.

I don't do classroom management. I am an instructional specialist. I don't deal well with behavior problems, nor am I the one to poke, prod, or coddle students who refuse to do work. It's just not my thing.

I am a person who likes to follow routines, but I have never been able to keep up any behavior modification routines I have ever started. It's just not me and I know why. I was raised old school. When grown folk told you to do something, you did it. When grown folk told you not to do something, you didn't do it. You went to school to learn and while you were there, you got your lesson. You did what the teacher said. If you didn't, there would be a problem at the house.

Because of this upbringing, I just can't understand or get on board with asking a child to do or not do something multiple times. If a kid wants to learn, I'm here for it. If a kid does not want to learn, that's his or her prerogative—but don't disrupt my class.

I can hear you all now!

"Teachers are supposed to love all students."

"It's your job to make them want to learn."

"Some kids haven't been taught at home, so you need to take the time to teach them."

Yep. All of that is correct. Still, I don't do classroom management. **shrugs**

I've taken all sorts of professional development workshops and trainings on how to manage student behaviors. I know the strategies. The problem is that managing negative behaviors is not authentic to what I believe in and that is why I have a hard time committing to it. Students can always tell when you are not being authentic!

Now I'm sure you're thinking that my classes must have been out of control. Nope. Not that either. I am an "instruction" person. My strong suit is planning engaging and fun lessons and incorporating a lot of lab time. I was able to manage behaviors indirectly by creating a classroom where learning was fun.

I also used a lot humor. Or, what I thought was humor. My students mostly thought I was lame and laughed for that reason, but I didn't care why they were laughing as long as they were having a good time.

Many students became like family to me. I remember one year having a group of students I affectionately referred to as "the lunch bunch". We'd gather every day in my classroom and eat together. Sometimes I'd bring food for some or all of them, and at other times they'd bring something for me. We may have ordered in a few times as well! All of my classes thought they were my favorite... and they were! One class was my favorite academically, another was my favorite creatively, and so on.

When you connect with students on this level, you don't need discipline. So, no, I don't do classroom management!

Confession #7: I was never interested in being a principal.

There is nothing about being a principal that I find exciting. True, I like being in leadership positions, but that is one that I do not desire. "You couldn't pour that on me," as they say.

I am a responsible person, but I don't like being held responsible for other people's actions, or lack thereof. Yes, there is some of that in teaching as well, but nowhere near to the same degree as having a whole building to be held accountable for. Could I handle it? Of course, I could, I think. But I don't want to find out. The bottom line is I just don't want to work that hard.

Confession #8: I preferred hanging out with the older teachers.

Most of my close friends are older than me. The majority of them are actually five or more years older than I am. I have always been drawn to older people. When I was a child, I preferred staying in the house with my mama, aunties, and grandmama over going outside to play. I guess it is because I like to learn, and people with more experience than you have a lot to share.

When I was teaching, I was the same way. I'd find the older teachers and link up with them. Boy did I learn some things!

Confession #9: I never fully trusted administrators (with the exception of one).

It wasn't until later in my career that I was finally able to work with a principal who I felt that I could trust, who appreciated and respected my talents, and that was truly interested in my growth as a professional. Up until that point, I handled administrators with a long-handled spoon. I "had a right to", in the words of my mama, because I'd been burned early on... like in my pre-career... as in my student teaching! No, no no... I'm not bitter. I just learned my lesson.

While I was student teaching I made the mistake of thinking that your administrators always had your best interest at heart. I took a job offered by the school where I student taught because I didn't want the hassle of looking for a position. Looking back I see that I was only operating in fear and resting in my comfort zone. At any rate, I buddied up with some of the teachers, including the department chair. The following year, when I was an actual teacher, I saw her for who she truly was. She only "respected" me when she thought I was one of them.

You see, this department functioned as a unit within content areas. For example, each biology teacher would take turns copying the unit. Yes, you read that correctly. They copied units. They had folders. The folders contained teaching units for each standard. There were worksheets, quizzes, and the occasional lab. Any projects, which were few and far between, were also in the folder.

When it was your turn to "plan", you simply took the folder and made sure that you made enough copies of everything for all of the teachers in your content area. You then took a blank calendar and filled in the dates that each "lesson" would take place. Finally, you distributed this about a week in advance so that the other teachers had time to go over the worksheets and make answer keys which the entire team would review together. I'm not sure why they didn't just copy those from previous years too. I mean, biology changes, but not that quickly.

After the first couple of units, I was done! I told them that I wanted to actually plan engaging lessons, use technology, and do more labs and if no one wanted to do it with me, I'd do it by myself. I confirmed that we were not required to "plan" together so that I would not be in violation of any district rules. I went my own way and did my own thing.

The other teachers did not like it, but my department chair said she thought I had great ideas and she welcomed the originality. Tuh! At the end of the year, in my formative evaluation, I was told that I was not a team player and that I might be a better fit at a school that does not value collaboration as much as they did. Were they kidding me? I was told I'd be reassigned due to a reduction in force. I packed my duds and gladly left.

Fast forward about seven years later, said department chair showed up at my school, the one I was reassigned to, as an assistant principal. Needless to say, the mistrust was already there and we did not "set horses". Ultimately, she was involved in an incident with the principal, where grades in my online gradebook were being changed. Lowered in fact.

The grades of a student whose parent was also a district employee. A parent, in front of whom, I did not bow down to during a conference with the assistant principal and principal. Each day the mother would check the grades online and each day the student was coming back with printed grade reports where a 77 had been changed to a 75 ,or a 89 had been changed to an 86. Small differences, but with enough of them, her grade dropped significantly. I knew that I had not done it so I immediately reached out to the IT department to open an investigation.

Initially, the investigation was opened and I was told I'd have a list of all IP addresses that had accessed my gradebook by the end of the week. I never got it. I also never got another call back, another response to an email inquiry. Nothing. In fact, I was called in for a meeting. When I asked the nature of the meeting I was told that it could not be discussed prior to the meeting. (Side Note: Always ask if the meeting is a disciplinary matter. If they don't want to tell you, assume that it is and union-up!)

At that point I knew it was time to call for legal representation from my professional organization (Georgia does not allow actual unions). The assistant principal and principal were completely defensive and questioned why I was even trying to find out who changed the grades. Why wouldn't I want to know? Especially given the history of my relationship with the parent. Long story short, I left.

Every school that I worked in after that, I kept my distance from administrators as much as possible. If they didn't say nothing to me, I didn't say nothing to them. I didn't care about getting promoted so I felt as if I didn't need a relationship with them.

Turns out when you become a consultant you kind of do need pre-established relationships, but that's okay! As far as I was concerned, I had no love for administrators beyond the scope of my job duties. That is until my last position with my last principal. She was so amazing that I'll have to write about her another time!

Confession #10: I believe there are some tried and true, old school strategies that should still be used today.

If it ain't broke don't fix it. Some things just don't need to change. If something has worked for years and years, how does it all of a sudden become ineffective?

I firmly believe in adapting and adjusting. You read my long story about the folders, so this is not an attack on new instructional strategies. It is an attack on throwing out babies with bath water, as the old saying goes. Having a new way to capture a student's attention should not automatically disqualify a method that has been around for years. Call me out of touch, but I still believe that spelling, grammar, and punctuation should matter at all times.

I believe that students should still have weekly vocabulary in every class. There should still be vocabulary quizzes on Fridays, and spelling should count. I still believe that students should have to do homework. I also understand the reasons why some oppose it, however, homework works when properly administered. I don't see anything wrong with posting a student's grades with their name next to it. Can it be embarrassing if they don't do well? Yes! Does it also motivate kids who are doing well to continue to do well? Surely, does!

Anyone who attends a workshop with me will tell you that I am highly engaging with lots of activity. I also believe though, that sometimes learners need to just sit down and focus. I'm saying all of this to say, we didn't get here by accident. The methods that our teachers used produced some pretty amazing people. Why get rid of it all? Why not tie it into what we are doing today to even further enrich the learning experiences of students?

Confession #11: I like my freedom more than I like being in the classroom.

As much as I loved teaching, I like my freedom more. I like being able to make phone calls when I need to and being able to go to establishments that close at 4:00 p.m. on a weekday. I also like being able to go to the restroom as frequently as necessary. I can go wherever I want for lunch. Hell, I get to eat lunch!

Confession #12: I don't mind standardized tests.

Let's give standardize tests all day long! The problem is not the testing, but the fact that teachers are required to teach one way and assess another. If I teach using problem-based learning, then I should also assess using problem-based learning. This is a simple concept, not at all hard to grasp. You can ask for rigor and real-world scenarios all year long then test students over a bunch of random facts on a multiple-choice test. It just doesn't make any sense.

I'm not saying teach to the test either. I am saying teach the material that will be on the exam. Show the students multiple ways to reason the same answer. If a district requires performance-based assessments throughout the school year and students have had little interaction with the vocabulary for the course, it is unreasonable to expect them to know that vocabulary at the end of the year.

Conversely if students have spent ample time learning vocabulary, how and when to use it, and the various contexts in which it might appear, then standardized test questions for those terms can vary from what they have previously seen and they should still be able to show mastery. Assessments have to be both valid and reliable in order to give a good measure of what students have learned. A portion of that is based on the assessment actually assessing what has been taught.

We also need to use standardized test data more responsibly. As it currently stands, different states have different rules regarding which students are required to test. Data that is given in sound bites is not reflective of the fact that one state tests ALL students, even those who do not speak or read the language in which the test is written, while another state may only test their gifted and honors population. There are also a lot of other factors that are ignored. Yes, data is reported by sub-groups, i.e. socioeconomic status, gender, ethnicity, etc. but data does not account for those who are impacted by trauma or have other issues that impact their learning.

Confession #13: I don't miss the classroom!

I can honestly say I don't miss being a teacher, at least not in the traditional sense of working for a school district. I don't miss having someone else determine what time of day I can eat. I don't miss having someone determine if it is okay for me to use the restroom. I don't miss having someone rearrange my day by announcing an impromptu faculty meeting.

I miss helping students realize that science is not that hard. I miss the insightful conversations that I used to have with my students. I miss the creative process of coming up with a new project-based learning experience and the excitement that came when it was time to introduce it to students. I miss being a teacher.

These are my confessions!

"You may encounter many defeats, but you must not be defeated. In fact, it may be necessary to encounter the defeats, so you can know who you are, what you can rise from, how you can still come out of it." - Maya Angelou

2

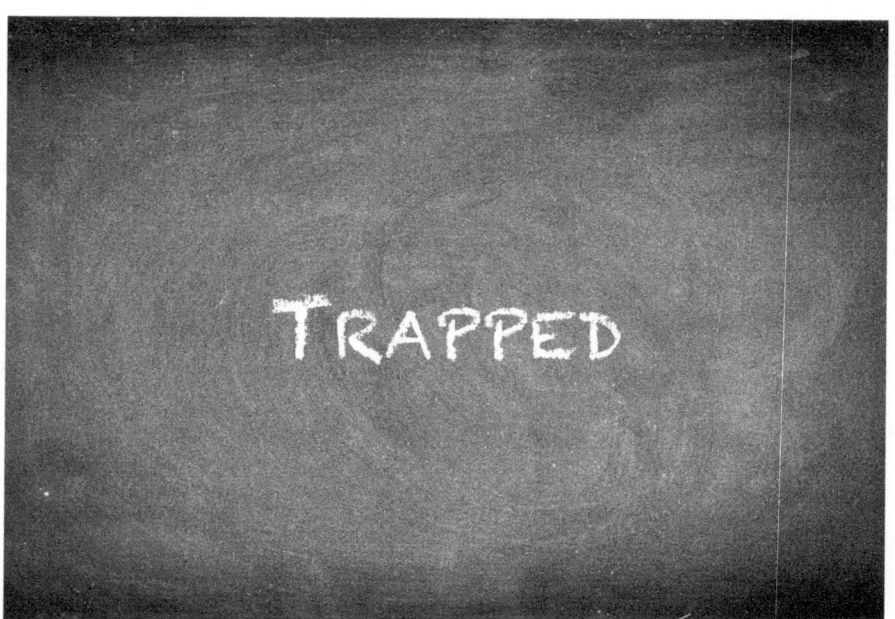

by Dr. Ragan M. Brown

The alarming truth is that many educators are stuck in their classrooms. They feel trapped in a profession that was designed to be rewarding. The 2017 Educator Quality of Work survey findings illuminated the ongoing stress and burnout an educator endures. In fact, of the 5,000 surveyed, 61% reported that their work in education was either always or often stressed.[1]

Although I wasn't a participant in that study, I am no stranger to the mediocrity trap. It's a loss of motivation and loss of enthusiasm in the classroom. Mediocrity eloquently trapped me like a Venus fly trap ploys its prey. Slowly I slid into the trap and I chose to hide for years in a dark well or dungeon of a classroom, alone and in silence.

The feeling of entrapment is terrifying and it feels like there is no place to run. Sadly, thousands of educators experience this feeling. The time has arrived to rise up and break the chains of mediocrity. Trapped educators need to understand that they are not suffering alone. Therefore, the following stories are cries of help that weren't heard and overlooked. Maybe you are the trapped educator in these stories as well. Unfortunately, I was the trapped educator in these stories. Same story, different educator.

Trapped Educator Story #1

The bell rings and now it's show time! The Teaching Show! My students had no idea that I was suffering. Like clockwork, I greeted them at the door, helped them to get settled, listened to the pledge, prayed through that moment of silence, dismissed them to first period, and began my daily shenanigans of mediocrity.

Then I walked into my classroom, the dark hole. Although, it was filled with color, laughter, aligned lesson plans, student engagement, and most of the time progress, there was still a darkness and sadness that existed. I was an expert at hiding it. My insides felt like a ring of fire.

Trapped Educator Story #2

As the alarm clock glared at me, we began to play a game of cat and mouse. Day in and day out, I extended my arm, turned away, and buried myself in comfort and security. For at least three years I engaged in this game. How I wished the buzzing, beeping, beating, and booming, would go away and bother another person.

A moment of question: Have you had an ongoing boxing match with the alarm clock lately? Not the occasional snooze button tap, but an ongoing, pattern of tap, turn, cover, tap, turn, cover.

Trapped Educator Story #3

Nothing I did could stop the feeling of not wanting to wake up and face another day in education. At one point, I set the alarm at 4:30 a.m. to get a jumpstart. Trust me it was all planned out. Private time with God, workout, shower, eat breakfast, get ready, and out the door. Honestly, it worked!

Trapped Educator Story #4

Finally with 30 minutes to spare, I would take a shower, get dressed, barely eat breakfast, comb my hair, toppling over invisible things because I was moving frantically, quickly, and carelessly throughout my home. Daily, I felt like a contestant in something that resembled a Minute to Win It Challenge. At last, I would dart out of the door, and insert myself into the steady commute to the dungeon of unhappiness—my classroom. Tears consumed my face at least three to five days of the work week.

A moment of question: Has your daily routine been a never ending race for the door cycle?

Trapped Educator Story #5

As I parked my vehicle with five minutes to spare, I began the trudge to my classroom (the dark side). I masked the wildfire. During that walk I transformed into a firefighter and put out the inner flames of sadness, guilt, defeat, and severe burnout.

No one knew what was occurring on the inside. The one with the biggest smile, no one would ever suspect. Praying my way up the stairs, dragging my feet as I turned left down the hallway, another left down, and into the dark side. How ironic that a class with so much color and life was actually a place of gloom.

Constantly thinking to myself, there has to be a way out. This is not life. Somedays I hoped to be fired. Believe or not, I truly felt that way. There were days when the lesson plans were blah.

And Then Mediocrity

Mediocrity trickles in, you begin to just get by and time either stands still or flies by. "The mediocre teacher tells. The good teacher explains. The superior teacher demonstrates. The great teacher inspires."

Still passionate, still making up songs, still striving to make a difference. Teaching until the bell rang. Staying after school to help with student projects. It appeared as I wasn't skipping a beat.

Guilty! Guilty! Guilty!

Somedays I demonstrated, somedays I inspired, but the majority of years 3 and 5, I admit that I felt like I was just telling. If you walked into my classroom, you would never suspect it. It didn't appear that way, but it felt that way. It's embarrassing to say that teaching felt like a life without parole prison sentence. Trapped.

Feeling like there was no way out and simply living a life of hopelessness. I felt like I did a crime and served my time. I was merely surviving, like many mediocre teachers in classrooms. Persistence and perseverance, and put together, yes a vast majority of stellar teachers have bouts of mediocrity.

What's confusing is that I absolutely loved teaching, however it turned into a love hate relationship. This profession and the knack for making educational concepts come to life was slowly becoming.

It's not the students or the act of teaching, it's the OTHER stuff. The OTHER duties on the contract. It's the fact that you don't get a chance to teach! It's the burnout, it's the unrecognized grief, it's the hidden depression.

Early Detection and Awareness is Key

The signs were present long before I realized it. Retrospection has provided a window of time for me. At one point I couldn't stand the sound of my name. Ms. Brown, Ms. Brown, Miss, Ms. Brown.

Cringe.

Some people are sensitive to sound, I was sensitive to my name and talking. Rides home in silence were relaxing until overwhelming thoughts of my alarm clock going off the morning resurfaced. I was so frustrated and discombobulated, I gave an exam to the wrong class!

There were times when I remember one day I just sat in the middle of my classroom floor. The kids thought it was a part of the lesson. It was actually a mechanism for survival. I was telling them how to do something during science class as opposed to demonstrating or provoking inquiry.

Thankfully, my irritability didn't overpower me. That was probably the ultimate mediocre lesson I ever delivered. My emotions and mediocrity were a chemistry experiment waiting to explode... or burn.

Symptoms and Diagnosis

What is Teach-pression?

When you have time to reflect and think, you begin to see things differently. I self-diagnosed this period of time as Teach-pression. If this was an actual medical illness, it would be a hybrid of depression induced by the daunting overloading tasks educators endure. Negatively impacts your overall mood and mental stability in the classroom. Unfortunately it overtakes your personal physical and any glimmer of hope.

Year 3, 5, and 7 are sometimes reported as the years this occurs. Symptoms include: worthlessness, guilt, fatigue, loss of desire to design creative lessons, dazed and raged in meetings, improper sleep cycles, lashing out at others, carelessness, working late nights to catch up, weight gain, extreme melancholy, the inability to perform daily tasks, and life threatening burnout. In this case, the tasks associated with teach-pression is teaching.

Let's not get on the subject of coworkers. Thankfully I was blessed to have an amazing group of coworkers. We were all operating in teach-pression. Many of us were sick and tired of being sick and tired. We leaned on each other for support.

Know the Signs and Triggers of Teach-pression!

This feeling can be compared to a standstill in time and the vital decision to reset is necessary. Feelings of guilt because you are not meeting the needs of students in in your classroom. Sometimes it felt as though I was checked out.

Are you coasting?

Time to be honest: You are burnt out! Burnt out like ash from a fire. Seek help!

Effect: You are running on fumes to provide a stellar lesson.

Sign 1: You are sick, but you don't take the day off.

Sound familiar:

- It's just a headache, it will go away

- The students need... I have a... I'll just go to the urgent care on the weekend...

- Cough drops, tea, allergy meds, cough suppressants... it will go away

- Stomach pains from unhealthy snacking

- Not eating lunch

- Lack of sleep, dreaming about what was left undone

- Negativity takes precedence

Sign 2: No restrictions, No boundaries

- You seem to think you are superwoman or superman

- Your living room looks like a paper warehouse

- You have 20 million tabs, sticky notes, lesson ideas posted in various places

- Ungraded papers are tucked away under a pillow in your home

- You are usually up at 3 o'clock in the morning working on schoolwork

- You agree to several extracurricular activities for your school

- Impossible expectations

Sign 3: The constant feeling that someone is watching you and there is a target on your back

- Feelings of scrutiny are magnified

- Feeling like your lessons are dissected

- Your family tells you that something is different

Sign 4: Someone please come and rescue

- Work piles up on your desk

- You don't feel supported, in actuality the administrators are probably burnt out as well

- Inattentive in meetings

- The school district seems reactive as opposed to proactive

- One new initiative after another

- Lack of support for behavior intervention

- Pressures of the test overwhelm your

The Teach-phinany

At some point we all experience a revelation or an awakening. Think of this as a revolution or a change. During this pivotal period of time, your survival is at stake. I have since called this a TEACH-PHINANY.

I remember my teach-phinany vividly. I was sitting in a meeting and it felt like an outer body experience. It is a signal grasp of reality through something (such as an event) usually simple and striking.

I didn't pay attention intently, the first time or the second time. Instead, I put band aids on a few things, and kept living my life. The final time, yes, three times a charm happened on the last day of school. In that moment, I was forced to pause and hit the reset button.

As the time after this teach-phinany progressed, I realized everything I did was purposeful, intentional, life changing, and time sensitive. The same care and approach I used with my unmotivated students, now applied to me.

It's TIME for an AWAKENING: Road to Recovery

Disclaimer: I'm not that kind of doctor, so there is no way that I can provide or write a prescription. The only doctor's orders that I am issuing is a proactive approach. I was the trapped educator. Thankfully, the Teach-phinany worked in my favor. Although I allowed myself to get to the lowest point, I was able to turn back the clock and reset.

I suggest a simplistic approach. The 5 R's worked wonders for me. My suggestion is take what you need as you begin this road to recovery.

Revisit

- Take a moment to be aware of your present state.

- Be true to yourself. If you are a journaler, revisit those journal entries, seek guidance, go to Scriptures, go to a counselor.

- Go deep into reflection. Go back to your reasons for teaching, go back to your teaching philosophy, go deep into prayer and meditation.

- Create a list of inner improvements.
- Renew and Recharge.
- Sleep.
- Take time to restore your energy.
- Cleanse and detox. Your mind, spirit, career, and students will thank you later.

Redefine and Realign

- Create your own realistic Utopia.
- Realign and reorganize your professional goals.
- What would you like your teaching career to look like?

Revitalize and Recover

- Practice mindfulness... I am here for a purpose. I am ready to teach.
- Try something new.

- Carefully choose where your energy should be directed.

- Pick yourself up.

- Dust yourself off.

- One day at a time.

Responsibility

This is very simple. You have a responsibility.

Prevention and Management

Feeling Burnout? Feeling like you are stuck in a mediocrity time capsule? Be practical. Small changes yield progress. Burnout is sometimes inevitable, however it is manageable. It should not get to the point where you are complete ash. Put out those small fires before they become big fires.

You may slip into mediocrity, but you need to have plans in place to... Reclaim your TIME... Thank you Mrs.

Maxine Waters. These words take on so many meanings, but they are necessary.

Here are some ways to prevent and manage slipping into mediocrity:

It's time to adjust your thoughts and actions.

1. There is power in the your words. Be careful of whom you're listening. Tell yourself it's time to get back on track.

2. Say NO! You can't do it all.

3. Ask for assistance.

Adjusting my thoughts and words were my first order of business. Ranting Ragan was no longer welcomed in my space. I started putting myself first and asked for help when needed. Reciting affirmations and posting positive words on sticky notes helped to retrain and adjust my brain. Notes were in my desk, on my computer screen, in filing cabinets, in data binders, and notebooks for meeting. It was at the point where I had positive reminders on my phone to get through the school day.

Divide your time.

1. Three strikes you're out... However you decide to look at it, 3 should be your cut off: 3 habits in the morning; 3 close outs at night; 3 things to tackle at work. Only do three things.

2. Throw away the excessive to-do list. You can't do it all or please everyone.

My time was stretched like a rubber band. From lesson plans to paper work to after-school activity, I did way more than what was required of me. Committing to so many things overwhelmed me. After the teach-phinany, I had to minimize my to-do list to three things. My commitment list soon dwindled when I started to value my time. Writing down three things and crossing them off the list was much more fulfilling than having a million and one things that are not getting done.

When I finally escaped the trap, I learned how to use the one touch rule in the mornings before class began. If I touched it once, and I could do it quickly, I did, and it wasn't added to my to-do list.

Another change I made was choosing no more than two days to work later to get ahead for the next week. When everyone is gone, you get a lot of lesson plans and data analysis done. My headphones and music were my best friend on those days. I was amazed at how much work got done. I also had a chance to plan for interruptions.

Take time to listen.

1. Listen to your body.

2. Listen to your thoughts.

3. Get an outside opinion and collaborate.

I learned to listen to the warning signs from my body, especially when I felt pressured and overwhelmed (especially during testing time). When I took time to listen to what I wrote in my journal, it provided evidence that I needed to slow down. My journal often gave me the permission I needed. Quiet moments are a necessity for me. When I saw the patterns from what was written in my journal, my perspective transformed.

Do other things with your time.

1. Get a hobby.

1. Don't waste time picking the wrong battle.

2. Update your resume, maybe it's time for a career change.

The school day and work day goes by faster when you are having fun. I went back to incorporating extremely engaging lessons. Realizing that my time was precious and it was time to work smarter made a huge impact on my life.

Working out was my escape and kept me happy. I no longer allowed myself to be a prisoner of my classroom. I over-scheduled "me time" and left early. Investing in a spa membership was the absolute best thing I did.

On weekends, I explored ways to be a better me, as well as explored ways to transition to another grade level or career. Most people work out to get fit physically. My workouts were strictly for endorphins. I even started a mini herb garden with rosemary and mint to keep me focused.

Take time off.

1. Slow down. This is a great way to regroup and refocus.

2. Take a vacation day (Mental Health Day); if you are burnout, then you are sick.

3. Put the phone down! Unplug. The phone is sensory overload.

4. When I got comfortable with managing and preventing my burnout, I became bold and creative. I literally laugh each time I think of it. (Insert sly smile and laughter).

I remember giving myself permission to take a mental health day because my motivation was low. So I had this crazy idea to have a reason to schedule a substitute teacher. At the beginning of the year I looked up one of those unusual national holidays. The date I chose was October 1, the start of my birthday month and it was also National Homemade Cookies Day. In fact, I can still smell those chocolate chip with pecans and my attempt at chocolate mint cookies that filled my home.

It felt so good to be off, I did it again in February, anticipating another potential burnout. I remember taking off February 26 for National Fairytale Day. This was perfect, because coincidentally, I am passing my story down to you. The lesson here is take the time off. You are entitled to those days. Start looking at your "national holidays" during the summer and get the your sub plans ready. I created National "My Paperwork is Piling Up" day!

Sure I felt guilty, but I did not want to go back to the dark place that held me for so long. I began to realize if I gave all of me, then there was none of me left. It was imperative that I recharged in order to give my 110% to my students.

Time to switch it up.

1. If you procrastinate... Stop

2. If you complain... Stop

3. If you need to change grade levels, schools, districts, audience... Do it

4. If you need to change something... Stop and Switch it up

Going through a period of burnout is difficult. Sometimes things just don't work. At times I tried the same thing over and over, until I had to verbalize that I was making a change. When you are engulfed in work and life is passing by like cruise ships, you have to act quickly. I no longer allowed the environment to trap me.

I began to teach in the moment, live in the moment, and be mindful of my present moment. Switching up my classroom, holding class outside more often, making my lesson more engaging and interactive, and asking for help were a few of the best things I did to switch things around.

Setting aside 5-10 minutes before, during or after school allowed me to be reflective and hone in on what needed to be refreshed. Believe me, it helps prevent the burnout. If it weren't for reflection, then I would have been trapped in the same school district, not realizing that my time there was served.

Time to push through.

1. It's not easy, but it's intentional.

2. It's not quick, but it's consistency.

3. It won't change until you make a change.

Sure easy for me to say right? Pushing through is a choice. Are you going to stay stuck or push your way through and out of this temporary trap? Reflecting on why I started teaching in the first place gave me a renewed perspective.

Maybe I was simply trapped in the wrong classroom or the perhaps trapped teaching the wrong subject. Could it be possible that my positive outlook on life was confined? Renewing my perspective helped me grasp, that teaching was my calling and I should continue to pursue it.

In an effort to push through this trap, I had to restructure my routines. Even though things sometimes spiraled out of control, my routines remained the same. Each decision I made was intentional and for the greater good of me.

The final thought I would leave for you is this: Rediscover what makes you happy in teaching.

"You can't stay in your corner of the Forest waiting for others to come to you. You have to go to them sometimes." - A.A. Milne, Winnie-the-Pooh

3

by Melody A. Herb

Mental Health Day is what it's called. So overwhelmed. Can't think. Here I am again. Monday morning. Can't do it. Memories of last week and countless other weeks still in my head. If I was at school—at the job I love—this is how it would go down.

Who is in in-school suspension today; must stop what I'm doing to gather work for them, could be three or four students. There goes an hour. There goes my first period, which I used for preparation.

Phone rings. "Can you cover for Ms. Smith now?" Not like I can say 'no', it's in the contract. Rush to cover. Bring laptop. Arrive, set up class, begin to access emails.

"Please bring work to the guidance office for John Jones, who will be suspended out of school for two weeks." More work for me—another hour—the kid gets in a fight—he gets a vacation from school—I get to make a neat little package—ASAP mind you—of class assignments for him that I will never see again because he won't do it.

More emails—why is Susan failing your class? BECAUSE SHE DID NOT DO ANY WORK!! Another one—please fill out this form about Jennifer; have you seen any signs of drug use, depression, not wanting to go home, anger towards other students, etc. WELL I SURE HAVE—and if I tell you all of the things I've heard from other students (hearsay in a court of law), you'll make me get on the phone with Children & Youth services and that will take up the rest of my day. I love these kids—I give them lunch money and coats in the winter. Please don't doubt my commitment here.

Days like this stretch into weeks, months and years until something snaps and we read a story like this in the news: "A lifelong educator who no doubt was born with the unique qualities only a teacher can possess. He took his own life shortly after his name was published in the Los Angeles Times under the dreaded category of Ineffective Teacher." [2]

****

It has to stop. But it won't, not any time soon. How did I get here? Why it seems just like yesterday I was living large. Working in a major corporation for 18 years. Ha! Corner office and a secretary. Flying all over the place.

Then, abruptly, cue frying pan in the face. Opioid epidemic in my own backyard. Frantic call from daughter, "Can you bail me out of jail, Mom?" HELL NO! WHERE'S THE BABY?

From that moment in 2001 until today, my husband and I have raised our granddaughter. Her mother did not remain in jail, however her lifestyle of drugs and all that goes with it remained unchanged for many years. I was able to go to court that very day sixteen years ago and obtain an emergency custody order.

Overnight, exploring my career options became my main focus. I couldn't fly all over the world now. I needed to raise my granddaughter. I tried to manage it for a while until that became overwhelming.

In 2003, the corporation I was working for was laying employees off. I was offered a monetary package to leave my job and take an early retirement. I had worked for that company for 18 years. I accepted the package to leave with mixed feelings. I was sad but relieved. Now I had to move forward with a new career. What could I do that would use my business talents and let me be home for my granddaughter? Ah HA! I'll become a teacher that looks like a piece of cake! Summers off, woo hoo! Little did I know.

Fifteen years later I reflect. No doubt every new teacher is determined to make a difference. We all come to work wanting to do our best in spite of the negatives. Like the time on the first day back from summer vacation—year two. All of the teachers at my small intermediate school were freaking out because none of the printers worked. There was a connectivity problem. I could fix that! I made the rounds and one-by-one reconfigured the printer settings on all of my colleague's computers. We were up and running and preparing for another school year.

I was everyone's hero for about an hour. I had other schools in the district calling me for directions. Apparently, it was a district-wide problem. Efficient, corporate-executive-me-turned-teacher, emailed the entire district with directions on how to get the printers online again. I was sure to get a raise and a promotion I thought. I'm working this teacher thing. Details on the news at 11—there was sure to be a parade for me! It's the Big Easy at 5:00, cue the trombones! NO—Cue frying pan in the face.

Phone rings. "Superintendent of Technology for the district here, did you send out this email telling everyone how to fix the printer issue?"

I responded, "Sure did! Proud of me sir? It was nothing, really. Glad to help. No problem. Sir? You still there?" Really angry voice, "Don't you ever do that again." No good deed goes unpunished.

Particularly frustrating was the time I went to a student's house to see if he was okay. I heard rumors that he was refusing to come to school. He was a shy, smaller than average ninth grader with some family tragedies under his belt. Too much for a kid to bear.

It was right before Thanksgiving and I felt compelled. After speaking with the father, I stopped by one day after school on my way home. Long story short, he returned to school. Not because of me, but it helped. The next day the principal promptly, abruptly and in no uncertain terms informed me that "we don't do that".

Okay, let me get this straight, I cannot make home visits... I cannot hug/pat on head/shoulder. Must give passing grade to student who has only attended class 10 times (I've learned that doctor notes make every shred of responsibility a student has disappear). Cannot give candy, cupcakes, snacks. Cannot preach or discuss God. Cannot discipline—they have an "Individual Education

Plan" (IEP), meaning the student has "modifications" to their classroom learning experience.

These students with the IEP often receive less work, smaller tests, less discipline, and attend classes having much lower expectations placed on them than other students. In many cases the students do not do better with modifications, they do worse. I've heard this situation referred to by other teachers as "learned helplessness". Students get used to having excuses made for them and they stop trying.

Teaching middle school a few years ago was very different from teaching high school. One of the big differences were the papers I had to correct. I had to pay more attention to what the students wrote more so than at the high school level.

One afternoon I was correcting worksheets for my 6th grade computer skills class. One paper caught my eye because there was writing on the back of it. I did not tell the kids to write anything on the back, so I turned it over and this is what I saw, "My Uncle is touching me, he is hurting me, please help me." I died inside.

I ran over to the classroom of the Spanish teacher. I knew that this young student was Hispanic, and that this teacher was close to her due to the student being in her English as a Second Language (ESL) class. I showed my colleague the note on the back of the paper. We cried. When we recovered our composure, we called the principal and the state Children and Youth Services and reported it.

Waiting until the next day to hear news was unbearable. The next day we learned that the entire family had moved out of their house the night before and left no clue as to where they went. I think about that child daily.

****

The Semi-Solution: I found one key to keeping myself motivated was to get to know my students—their interests and the way they learn. The ones who want to learn really need each and every one of us. To this day I have guilt that I was not able to help that young girl. I was so overwhelmed with getting used to my job that the students became the number two priority.

Years ago, a therapist told me with regards to my drug-addicted daughter, "She might not make it, but you have to." That's right, I have to. I have to make it, I have to cope, there are others to help.

I also look to role models. I am not the only person in the world who has gone through a rough patch. I am not the only individual who has been blamed for something I had nothing to do with. I look to the strong among us and to those who are no longer with us, and I pray—a lot.

****

Just recently while I was writing this chapter, there was a fight between two boys that began in my classroom. They were friends before this incident. I have a computer lab and they were watching basketball on YouTube. A verbal argument about who was a better basketball player escalated into a physical fight outside in the hallway.

I called the office and stayed with my class. I did not go out into the hallway to break up the fight. These two students have Individual Education Plans and are considered "emotionally disturbed", both are on probation for convicted offenses. All fights are punished with 10 days out of school suspension; however, these students only received 3 days out. The reason? It was the teacher's fault for allowing the students to watch YouTube!

I could not believe my ears. I never "allow" students to use the computers for non-educational purposes. As soon as I turn my back, they go to wherever they want on the internet. I waste countless hours of class time policing what they are watching. My pleas to the technology department to block YouTube and other sites have been met with opposition. They say they cannot block these sites because many teachers use sites like YouTube to show educational videos.

This incident was devastating to me until I remembered my promise to myself: Look to other strong ones. Rosa Parks, Nelson Mandela, Anne Frank, and others. They all had what I need right now.

I also thought of my father. He was a police officer who turned other corrupt cops in and suffered in his career for it. He stood his ground on injustice. The issues that these heroes faced were massive when compared to what happens to me on my job, however they are a source of inspiration that lifts me up to a positive place so that I can get up the next day and teach.

"You will miss 100% of the shots you never take."

-Unknown

4

by Dee Harris

How did I get here? The fact that I am fifteen years into teaching still amazes me considering that I never wanted to become a teacher. In undergrad, I started out as a biology major, with the hopes of applying to physical therapy school and having a career as a physical therapist.

I had never really been academically strong in math and science, so you can imagine, pursuing biology as my major was quite challenging for me. I passed the class with a 'D' which is still a passing grade (believe it or not). Everything in that class was over my head and I never felt like I knew exactly what I was doing.

Realizing that I probably made a mistake in selecting my major, I found myself re-evaluating what I wanted to do with my life. I always liked the social sciences—psychology, sociology, and human development always interested me.

The university that I attended didn't have psychology as a major, but as I was looking through the academic programs of study, I came across something that said, 'Family & Consumer Sciences Education.' I immediately went to the program office to ask questions. Family & Consumer Sciences included some of the social sciences that I liked. It's actually what used to be called 'Home Economics.' I thought, "Life skills... that's perfect!"

Continuing in conversations with advisors, I then had to decide which pathway I wanted to pursue—non-education or education. I immediately thought "non-education". I said to myself, "Well, I definitely don't want to be a teacher." I mean after all, I was always the one in school or in my group of friends that would always say, "I would never be a teacher."

Let's fast forward a little to when I met Ms. Allen who would tell me, "I really think you need to consider switching pathways and coming over to the education side. You have the personality to be in the school setting." I can just remember looking at her like she had horns coming out of her forehead! Well Ms. Allen, look at me now, I'm fifteen years in.

****

When I started my first year of teaching at the age of 23, I was scared, nervous, and just wanted everyone to like me. I was hired by the same school district from which I graduated. I remember receiving my contract and looking at the salary of $38,433.00. I literally started screaming out loud in happiness and was rolling around on the carpet in my parent's living room. I thought, "Yes, I made it. I'm making money!"

My first year of teaching was mediocre. I was still learning the craft of teaching as I was teaching. I was learning how to handle different personalities of high school students, colleagues, and parents. I mean after all, I was still learning about myself, too. What else would it be but mediocre? I was still "wet behind the ears" and a rookie. I had good days and bad days, and by the end of the school year I couldn't believe that I made it.

By the time I reached my fifth year of teaching, I was feeling the usual burn-out that many new teachers felt. By this time, I had attained my Masters of Education in Human Development and I was still teaching at the same high school in which I started my teaching career.

By mid-year I was done. I couldn't take it anymore. I literally couldn't take it anymore. I felt so much anxiety about going to work. I didn't like going, I didn't like some of the kids, and I didn't like what I was doing. So I quit. Yes, I literally resigned in the middle of the school year!

I still regret that decision today. Looking back now, I realize that I didn't have the proper support system. I also wasn't mentored by administration to know how to ask for help and seek advice so I wouldn't have to make such a rash decision. I literally panicked and said that I had enough.

I stayed in the education field and got a job as a Program Manager for a non-profit organization. Not too far into that role I started feeling like, "Oh goodness, what did I do now?" I had taken a pay cut by taking that job.

Back when I attained my Master's Degree, my salary jumped considerably while I was still teaching. I remember being at the new job and sitting at my desk thinking, "I just took a step backwards and I'm still miserable." Saddened by the amount of money I was making (or lack thereof), I sought out to get back into the schools. I was hired by a neighboring school district. I couldn't go back to the district that I left since I broke my contract by leaving during the school year.

I was hired in my new teacher position, I thought, "Okay, this time it will be different." My first year back in the classroom was a little better than before. I was a lot more comfortable with building relationships with my students and "being on stage" every day.

The challenges came in with the leadership of the school. During the second year at my school, a new principal was appointed. With the principal changing, the leadership of the school also changed. I was becoming even more comfortable in my environment. Our school really started feeling more like a family atmosphere. I was enjoying my classes and my students. I was also becoming more involved in the school and became a member of the School Leadership Team.

Joining the Leadership Team started opening my eyes to different roles in the school setting. I found myself thinking more and more about leaving the classroom. But once I found myself thinking about that I would say, "I don't want to be an administrator."

The administrator's role seemed so stressful. Many see it as, "Why wouldn't you want to be in charge?" I just saw it as, "These people in suits walking around delegating tasks to staff, and disciplining students..." Let alone, administrators are always at the school. I felt like they had no personal life.

My perspective began to change quickly once the economy crashed and our district was hit with furloughs and a hiring freeze. Everything was halted and worst of all, no pay raises! Suffering through staying at the same step on the pay scale for four years left me back at square one... feeling frustrated and looking for a new job. I said to myself, "Well, the only way for me to increase my salary is to get a position out of the classroom that pays more, so I guess I will have to become an administrator after all."

By that time I went back to school once again to obtain my administrator's credential. Seemed as if I was applying for jobs left and right! I even applied to jobs that I knew I wasn't qualified for, nor were really a good fit. I just needed to make more money.

Then one day it dawned on me to check teaching positions in other school districts that would still give me an increase in salary. Luckily, I found one. I interviewed for the position and was hired. My salary increased significantly. I thought, "I don't care what challenges come with this school because I am finally making the salary I should be making based on my years of experience and education."

At that point, I was teaching at my third school in my third school district and I was finally getting paid my worth. Then why do I, yet again, have the feeling of "Is the classroom for me?" Why do I keep coming back to this place?

The Politics

Education is all about politics and money. Of course every district has its motto of how they are going to provide top notch education for all students and no student will be left behind. That, in theory, sounds good, but it's just not true. One reason I keep coming back to this place is because of the politics of teaching. With all of the state and county mandates, it is impossible to do just that... TEACH!

The public school system is inundated with testing requirements. There is some form of a test being administered literally from October through June of any given school term. That is basically the entire school year. Teachers are left feeling overwhelmed, trying to hit every major concept in the curriculum to make sure students are ready for testing. Having these constraints leaves little room for teachers to be as creative and more relaxed in their teaching style because everything is on a time constraint.

Then you have the politics of funding. Being a Career and Technology Education (CTE) teacher, we often feel the slight of when budget cuts come around. Many school districts have already eliminated vocational technology classes completely. I think this is sheer craziness! I mean, how can educators not see the value of these courses teaching everyday life skills?

On the flip side of not having enough funding for various programs within Career and Technology Education is the total disrespect we receive when our classes are treated as "dumping grounds" for "those kids"—you know the kids people think are not going to amount to anything in life. It is extremely frustrating when you are doing everything you can to market your program, engage students, and provide valuable resources for success only to have a colleague undermine your efforts.

How can we continue to chant all of these mottos for educating our youth but go on to do things that completely contradict the motto? We keep saying things like "Each one, teach one", and "It's about the kids", or "The students come first", but being in this profession I get a constant daily reminder of how that just isn't true. So to say the least, the politics of education constantly has me wondering, "Is the classroom for me?"

The Social Media Generation

I can definitely say my mediocrity in teaching throughout the last couple of years is definitely attributed to the social media generation. Students are more concerned with seeing how many "likes" or "followers" they have on their social media platforms. They walk into the class glued to their mobile phone; and when you are trying to start the class to teach, they are just sitting there scrolling through their media pages. So thus begins the battle of "put your phone away" or "let me have your attention" or "I'm not going to keep repeating myself". In addition, this behavior detracts from the students who are ready to learn and who want to be engaged, but have to put up with the constant distractions of students who just come to school to "hang out".

Of course I use social media to my advantage in my teaching practices, but there has to be a balance, especially since teachers are constantly reminded to differentiate instruction. A challenge is continuously coming up with the most creative ways to keep your students engaged and focused. I also find myself attempting to educate students on how to use their social media platforms for positivity, and for them using their voice to advocate for various issues. Just like technology, us teachers have to keep finding a way to re-invent ourselves to reach our students.

****

I think it's time to do something else in the education industry...

My frustrations recently have me feeling that it is time for me to consider another role in the education industry. I do love working with my students and helping students reach their full potential, but I also feel I am ready to teach in a different capacity. I've thought about going into Administration, but the more and more I think about it, I don't really believe that would be the best fit for me. I haven't completely ruled it out, but I want to explore options in which I think I would be the most impactful.

I've been thinking a great deal about consulting and/or having a Learning Center. I have even thought about leaving the profession altogether, but I always come back to the fact that at this juncture in my life, I've invested too much time and money to get to where I am. I know there are a plethora of different paths I can explore within the education industry; I just want to make sure the next phase of my career is serving a true purpose.

I don't want to catch myself saying, "What are we really doing?", or "What is the purpose of all of this?" These are statements I say quite often in my role as a classroom teacher. I love that I can control the constraints of my four classroom walls, but that is only to a certain extent. There will always be the "higher-ups" and the "powers-that-be" who make the decisions mandating what we have to do within those four classroom walls. The most frustrating aspect about that is many of those individuals never stepped a foot inside of a classroom. Again, this leads me to explore what can I do in the next phase of my career that will provide solutions to the issues that I have discussed? My hope is that I will move into a role that continues to be impactful in a positive way, and one in which I will not feel that I am doing a disservice to the students.

I would like to think the next phase of my career would be training new teachers who are coming into the education industry and/or running a learning center for children. I'm not sure if I've reached my glass ceiling as a mediocre teacher. Some days I feel that there is way too much work to be done within these four classroom walls, and then other days I feel like, "I just need to service these children in a different capacity".

My dream job would most likely be some sort of educational consulting. Becoming a Family & Consumer Sciences teacher has led me to explore the possibility of consulting families in exploring the benefits of enrolling in vocational programs. I definitely know that whatever I do next within this industry, I want it to be meaningful and have an intentional purpose.

"To the weak became I as weak, that I might gain the weak: I am made all things to all men, that I might by all means save some." - 1 Corinthians 9:22 (KJV)

5

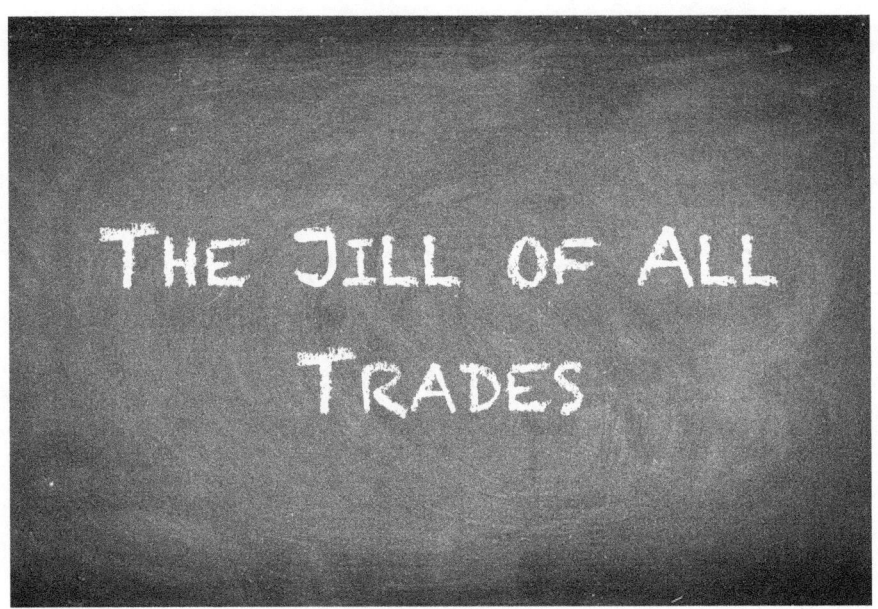

The Jill of All Trades

by Minister Ranyel L. Trent

"This was NOT in my job description!" Those were the words that raced through my head as I rushed to the girl's restroom with a hair brush, gel, and rubber bands in tote. This was the third time this week that I had to play hairdresser to a student whose drawstring ponytail kept falling out during Physical Education class.

I was dead smack in the middle of my planning period. My personal refuge from a day of being the referee of a boxing match, the mediator of an ensuing catfight, the counselor of puppy love gone wrong, and the schoolhouse mom of the kid who just needed that extra attention. Oh, and I almost forgot... AND TEACH!

So how dare she, a 4th grade child suffering from severe low self-esteem, have the nerve to be in a crisis in the middle of my planning period? However, at that point, it didn't even matter anymore because I learned that being a teacher clearly did not involve only teaching. It involved being anything that child needed in order to help that child succeed. As a teacher you have to be... the Jill of all trades!

CNN News reporter, Heather Sinclair Wood affirms that it does not matter how much you think you are prepared, you are never truly prepared for what the actual classroom will be like.[3] The average classroom size is approximately 23 students. This means 23 different personalities, 23 different backgrounds, 23 different attitudes, 23 different learning styles, and 23 different sets of parents. The moment you think that you finally got one student figured out, you realize that they changed on you.

I found myself having to be a mother to the students who lacked consistent motherly presence, and a singer/rapper to the student who could only comprehend through music. I had to become a game show host to the students who behaved better when taught through small group and center rotations, and a drill sergeant to the students who had no excitement about school whatsoever. I learned to always have a few rabbits in the hat for whatever type of day life may have thrown at me.

By the end of my final year in the classroom I felt like that of Apostle Paul in the Holy Bible (1 Corinthians 9:19-22) as I interpret it: I had become everything to every child so that I might help some.

I quickly learned that the art of adequate teaching was not found in the methodology or pedagogy you employ, but in the relationships you build. By becoming familiar with the things that your students are interested in will help foster a more positive classroom culture because now you can relate to them. I would often take the popular songs of the year and rewrite them into academic songs to help my students learn specific content information. They loved it because they were familiar with the rhythm and vibe of the song, and the fact that their teacher had actually listened to something they listened to.

Rita Pierson, a 40-year educator veteran, calls it 'being a champion'. In her 2013 speech on TED Talks she affirmed, "Every child deserves a champion; an adult who will never give up on them, who understands the power of connection and insists that they become the best they can possibly be." 4

****

Being the Jill of all trades doesn't mean that you have to be perfect at anything. It simply means that you are familiar with everything. It means that you can lend a helping hand when needed, whether it is with instruction, discipline, or administration.

For instance, my first six years of teaching was at the kindergarten level. However, I volunteered to help with 3rd grade after-school tutorials. No, I didn't know the 3rd grade curriculum as well as I knew the kindergarten curriculum. And no, I wasn't abreast on all of my mathematical computations to the point where I could teach it back effortlessly. But what I did possess was the knowledge of the basics and the courage to ask for help when needed. I knew how to switch roles when necessary.

As a Jill of all trades, you will often find yourself being placed in a position to learn something new or teach something back. You may find that you are asked to mentor other teachers or to lead a professional development on student relationships. This is not something to feign over or to become overwhelmed by. This is merely evidence of the impact of your many trades.

I remember one year I joked around with my class and re-wrote Kevin Gates' (a famous rapper) song, I Don't Get Tired, as a theme song for our test preparation season. The students all over were chanting the song and many of my students were asked to recite it over the loud speaker for the entire school to hear. That was an amazing opportunity not only for my students, but also for me to bridge my love for writing music with my love for teaching. It was a win-win situation.

Yet, little did I know that the next year and the year after that, and the year after that my principal would be asking me to write a new test prep song for the school. It was challenging some years, and many times I felt as though it was just one more thing on my long list of things to do as a teacher.

Teach them! Motivate them! Encourage them! Push them! Prepare them! The list seemed to never decrease until the end of the year and even then there would be a check-out checklist to complete before I was released. But, although I got frustrated with the demands that came along with being a Jill, nothing could replace the joy I felt when I watched my kids chant their song. It was pure rejuvenation knowing that my work was not in vain and that somebody somewhere needed me to bless them.

Take my school son for example, for the purposes of this book we shall call him... Johnny. I just happened to run into Johnny (literally, he ran dead into me) at the end of his first stint in 4th grade. He was not in my class, so I was not very familiar with his story. As I saw him running down the hall, I put on my disciplinarian hat and said in my stern southern Louisiana accent, "Baby, stop running in this hallway!" Immediately he halted with balled up fists and tears in his eyes.

I knew then in that moment that Johnny didn't need discipline, but rather a counselor. I gently asked what was wrong and discussed different ways he could have handled his anger. I took him for a walk with me until he cooled off. It just so happened to be my planning period AGAIN!

For the remainder of that school year, every time Johnny got upset in class his teacher sent him to me for cooling off. Johnny and I developed a bond that year. I would make visits to his house if he ever missed school. I would pick him up on Sunday mornings to go to church with my family. I would even keep snacks in my desk for him just in case he came to school hungry and angry. I would do all of these simple things because it established a trust factor between us and allowed me to be his teacher. You see, I understood Johnny, and I was willing to be what he needed when he needed it. I was willing to be his Jill of all trades.

But please understand that the Jill of all trades is not some fictitious character who swoops in with a red cape with "I TEACH" embossed on the front and saves the day. Nor is she the Olivia Pope of the classroom handling every issue that arises seamlessly. What she is, however, is an educator dedicated to the teaching and reaching of the holistic child.

As an educator, you must understand the significance of the call upon your life. You were made for this. God has gifted you to be their teacher. This is written in the Holy Bible, Romans 12:6-8, King James Version as it reads:

[6] Having then gifts differing according to the grace that is given to us, whether prophecy, let us prophesy according to the proportion of faith; [7] Or ministry, let us wait on our ministering: or he that teacheth, on teaching; [8] Or he that exhorteth, on exhortation: he that giveth, let him do it with simplicity; he that ruleth, with diligence; he that sheweth mercy, with cheerfulness.

Now I don't know about you, but that sounds a lot like the life of a teacher to me! A teacher must possess familiarity with all of these gifts in order to be the change agent a child needs in their life. You will have to prophesy over their problems because you can see their potential even when they can't.

You will have to serve and cater to all of their learning needs and accommodations. You will most certainly have to teach them about the standards of life, such as hygiene, relationships, forgiveness and compassion, to name a few. You will have to encourage them when they fall and you will have to give them hope when the situation seems hopeless. You will have to lead them to make the right choices in life, and you will have to show mercy when they make the wrong ones.

Now point to that imaginary "I TEACH" on your chest and boldly say... I AM A TEACHER! I WAS MADE FOR THIS! You were made to make a difference. You were made to be a change agent. You were made to inspire and spark possibility in the lives of children everywhere. YOU were made for this.

And this became true in my life with my school son sooner than I had expected. After developing a really great rapport with Johnny the previous year, my principal thought it would be effective or maybe even humorous for him to be in my homeroom class the following school year.

However, apparently someone failed to inform Johnny that he had been retained. The very first day of the new school year Johnny zipped and zoomed through the hallways like a mad man screaming, "I'm supposed to be in 5th grade!" The assistant principal was already in pursuit in addition to a couple of paraprofessionals.

Now, a part of me wanted to just shut my door and pretend that I didn't hear anything, but the Jill in me made me walk out of the door and stop him. I managed to calm him down and get him to enter the classroom, but for the remainder of that year we fought, we cried, we loved on one another, and we wanted to literally choke one another.

There were days when Johnny wouldn't do anything in class but pick at his cuticles with his pencil before he fell asleep. I would leave him sleeping until Physical Education period, then I would keep him behind and help him with his work because, on that day, I was his personal tutor.

Other days he would get off of the bus angry, so our entire morning would consist of me putting out fires he tried to start with other kids. He would try to walk out of the classroom, but I would become a security guard blocking the door. Then at exactly 10:00 a.m., after he was considered present, I would move away from the door and allow him to walk out while whispering in his ear, "I will pass by your house after school to drop off your missed assignments."

By the end of the year, Johnny had passed 4th grade and received an award for most improved in math. His mom called it my teacher magic. But it was nothing magical about what I did with Johnny. There were no secret ingredients to getting him to perform for me. I simply cared enough about him to become what he needed me to be, when he needed me to be it.

That is what the Jill of all trades is truly about. It's not focusing so heavily on what is wrong with the educational system, such as how we are underpaid, underappreciated, or how we have no disciplinary support from administration; but it is allowing ourselves to be open enough to do what we can, when we can, and how we can. It is embracing every student as though they were birthed from our very own womb. It is acknowledging that we possess the power to create positive change in the world. It is reflecting on the purpose by which we all teach, and that is to make a difference in a child's life.

I know it will get frustrating at times. There will be moments in which you want to throw in the towel because it seems as though no matter how hard you try to help, the students don't seem to want to help themselves. I get it. I, too, have been there.

Trust me, there were many days when Johnny made me want to give up the career of teaching altogether. I wanted to straight put in my two weeks' notice and get a refinery job or something, but then I remembered the reason why I teach. It is not for fortune or fame. It is not for accolades or awards. It is not even for elite status or esteem. It is because I want to give every child the same opportunity I would like my children to have, an opportunity to become their very best.

So to all of my Jills, or Jacks reading this, will you answer the call? Will you become the confidant to the child with a secret? Will you become the voice of reason between two warring cliques? Will you become the friend to the child who is lonely? Will you become the role model to the child who needs someone to look up to? Will you become the Jill of all trades?

"Mediocrity is the companion of passivity and will not heed the call of great things."
- Craig D. Lounsbrough

6

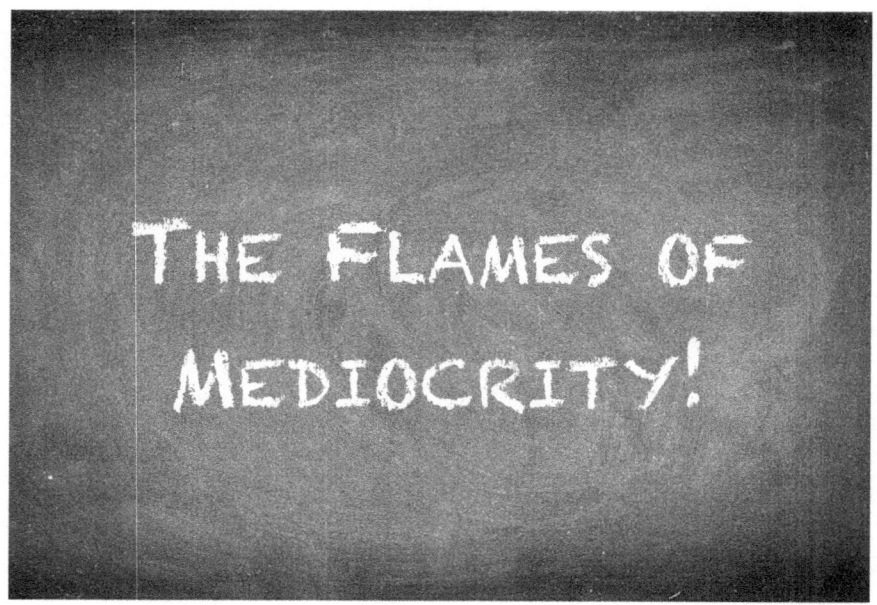

by Carole Cramer-Banks

There is an ancient Greek myth about a bird that lives hundreds and hundreds of years, and then after that it goes through a rebirth of itself. This bird is a phoenix and according to the Greeks, this bird never dies really.

Instead, when the phoenix thinks its come to the end of its long life, it sets itself on fire and is born again from its own ashes. Well, that's the short version of this Greek myth. But I have a point here and there's so much that can be learned from this bird.

Drawing a comparison between myself and the phoenix is elementary since the phoenix positions itself as the overseer on guard constantly watching for threats, seeking to find ways to overcome those things that would seek to destroy it. Right now, I am positioned to survey the land and see the whole picture. The ancient Greek myth of a phoenix has prepared me for the battle. Like the phoenix, I am now able to see the bigger picture and threats to myself. At this point, mediocrity was one of my biggest threats. I, like the mythical phoenix, have been reborn, regenerated, renewed and risen from the ashes to become a better, stronger version of myself.

****

Many times, over the years, I've died to self and been reborn. If you're doing anything worth doing, you have to, if not die to yourself, re-discover YOUrself over and over again. During the times that I've shed my old skin and been reborn and during the times when I was ash, I did not think that I would ever rise again. During those times, I felt completely broken. Little did I realize that at those times, I was being shaped and formed into the ME I would eventually become and love! Most importantly, I know the way to not only survive, but thrive.

In order to thrive and to be successful I knew that I had to make S.M.A.R.T. goals and stick to them. So, I made them and stuck to them. My definition of thriving included, first and foremost, not neglecting my family; secondly, I wanted to pass all of my classes at Loyola Marymount University (LMU) with a B+ or better; and thirdly, I wanted to be the best teacher I could be.

However, on the road to trying to be the best teacher, I ran into some bumps along the way. One of those bumps took the form of earning the ire of my former Principal. We did not have a good relationship since we did not understand each other. I'll say that my quirky little personality got in my way. I'm really not sure how everything really played out, but I'm guessing that she took one look at me and decided that she didn't like me.

That's how I imagined it happened. The truth could be so different but since I don't know what the "truth" is, I will stick with my version.

During my first year of teaching, I had no idea what I was doing. I struggled greatly. I was lesson planning day-by-day, not getting any sleep, and in survival mode. If you really want to laugh, I'll mention that I didn't even know that I had a Teacher's Edition (T.E.) with all the answers. I could go on, but you get the picture.

However, despite all of that, I did not consider my first year that bad. I had a goal to become the best Special Education teacher I could be. I decided that if I was going to do it, that I was going to do it right. I was going to rise through the ranks to become one of the greatest teachers because there's nothing mediocre about me.

So now, after just having said that, I am going to make a shocking confession! At one point I was a mediocre teacher! Why was I a mediocre teacher?!?! Well, I'm glad you asked. I'll answer that question by making the understatement of the year... nay, of the century when I say, "Teaching is not easy"! That is why it's not hard to be a mediocre teacher. At All. Let's unpack the definition of a mediocre teacher.

So, what is a mediocre teacher? According to Dr. Marquita Blades, "A mediocre teacher is one who is an overall GREAT teacher, who LOVES teaching, but also HATES going to work." How then, did I, at one point, end up being a mediocre teacher? Well, that's a long story. I only have a chapter to tell you about it, so let's begin.

****

Right now you may be wondering how I got to the point of being a mediocre teacher when my goal was to be one of the greatest? Well, it took a while for me to get to the point of being a mediocre teacher. At my best, I was still plugging away and doing my due diligence, trying to be the best teacher I could be. At my worst, I absolutely hated going to work, sitting in my car until the last minute. My rationale was that I was not getting paid any extra to be there early. If I was even one minute late, I would get a yellow line on my name, besmirching my record.

But this was only a part of my first year as a teacher. It seemed that my principal made it her personal mission in life to make my life hard. Any possible chance she could, she had something negative to say about me. Whenever she observed me, there was rarely ever any positive feedback; only corrective actions to be taken.

The problem, as I saw it, was that she wanted me to come into her office and talk to her about my daily teaching and experiences. Although many of the teachers took her up on her offer to come and talk, I did not. Because of what I considered the constant negativity, I did not let her in. I closed myself off to her and her attempts to pry into my life.

Of course hindsight is 20/20. Now, I can see that she was trying to help. But back then, I didn't like her leadership style and I pushed back. She pushed back as well. As you can imagine, things did not go well for me. I began to have stomachaches and the Sunday night blues. Despite all of that, I successfully completed my first year of teaching. I even managed to help raise my student's tests scores. I was so thankful for summer break.

Ashes to Ashes

"... Like a phoenix, she rose from the ashes!!!"

I came back from summer break somewhat refreshed. Even though I was near my breaking point, I kept pushing. I didn't know what was in store for me. If I thought that my first year of teaching was a challenge, it was nothing compared to my second year of teaching.

During my second year of teaching, I ran into another 'bump in the road' in my quest to be one of the best. That 'bump' was my first experience teaching someone with an Emotional & Behavioral Difficulties (EBD) disorder. That student was a force to be reckoned with. If he didn't like something, he tore the bulletin boards down, flipped over the desks, spit on other students, and even tried to choke other students. Yes, he tried to choke other students! I couldn't believe it.

That experience of teaching a student with EBD was something totally new to me. I had never experienced anyone trying to choke someone. I was so out of my depth and ready to quit. The only advice I was given was to document his behaviors so that, next year, he would be transferred to a non-public school (NPS). That little bit of advice was a small consolation for the daily stress that I and my students experienced.

Can I just say that documenting behavior does little to nothing to calm the fears of the other students who were afraid of the daily tantrums! I was completely overwhelmed but, since no help was forthcoming, I dealt with the erratic, violent tantrums as best I could until I simply could not deal with it anymore.

The final straw came when I broke my toe at home, in a totally unrelated incident. I usually stayed at work until 5:30-6:00 p.m. But, on that particular day, I was in so much pain because of the broken toe, that I went home early. Well, as it turned out, it was a good thing that I left work on time because the mom of the student with EBD sent her aunt to fight me! She would definitely had tried to fight me herself had she not been pregnant.

The reason she was upset and sending her relatives to fight on her behalf was because I didn't give her son any treats. It had a little something to do with him punching other kids and destroying the classroom. Why the mom couldn't accept that, I'm not sure. Now, that I've been around for a little while, I know a little better how to work with students with EBD. I would probably not respond the same way now. However, back then, was my first experience trying to teach someone with EBD and I was completely overwhelmed, burnt out, and unprepared. I melted down and burst into flames! Like the phoenix, I was dying so that I could rise from the flames and come back even stronger than before.

Rising from the Flames! (The Yellow Line of Despair!!!)

> "Returning from the flames, clothed in nothing but her strength, more beautiful than ever before."
> -Shannen Heartz

As if dealing with the student and mom from hell wasn't enough to make me melt down and burst into flames, I had to deal with the secretary from hell who seemed to really enjoy her yellow highlighter. I quickly learned that my work ethic and my results with my students didn't exempt me from the indignity of the yellow line!

Oh, that yellow line! I shall, now and forevermore, refer the yellow line as The Yellow Line of Despair! Seeing

The Yellow Line of Despair exactly one minute past sign-in time has the potential to mess up your day. What is The Yellow Line of Despair? The Yellow Line of Despair is the line the school secretary (or whoever is in charge of ensuring teachers are on time) puts across your name when you don't sign-in at the assigned time. For me, that time was 7:45 a.m.

Putting in the many hours of overtime that teachers do does not guarantee a pass from the school timekeeper when you're late. Nothing means anything when, even after all of the extra unpaid time put in, you see that Yellow Line of Despair across your name. No matter how hard you worked, there's always that Yellow Line of Despair to bring you down a peg or two.

Because of that yellow highlight across my name, I stopped caring as much; it broke me. Well... maybe it was just a symptom of the larger problem; but it was my breaking point. After all, as teachers, most of us give our ALL, day in and day out. Teachers are so willing to put that proverbial cross on our back, among other things, and carry it for as long and as far as we can for all it's worth. Why do we do that? Teachers are such martyrs. Why can't we just work our little 40 hours a week, stop spending money out of our own pocket, and be content with just being alright? Read mediocre!

I recall one time I came in early, walked past the secretary, spoke to her, and hurriedly rushed to my classroom forgetting to sign-in. Signing in was the last thing on my mind. What do you think I saw when I left for the day? Yep, you guessed it, The Yellow Line of Despair.

Are you kidding me? I was so done! I asked the secretary why she would highlight my name when I was one of the first teachers there. I reminded her that I spoke to her. She told me to sign in next time and it wouldn't happen. I tried to reason with her and let her know that I always come early, sign in, put in a little extra time and leave late.

To some, it may seem like I'm making excuses. After all, I am responsible for signing it, right? All I can say to that is deadlines—lesson plans due at work, assignments due at school. That's enough to burn anyone out. I just wanted some kind of help, at least one pass. C'mon, cut a sista' some slack! Do you think she did? Nope. None of that mattered to her. She wouldn't budge. I was ash!

Because of the incident with the mom from hell sending her aunt to fight me, I no longer felt safe, so I took a stress leave from work. So, in the midst of everything, I still had to raise my children and attend classes at LMU. I called into work everyday as required, but did not have plans to return because I worked next to a dangerous housing project and I did not feel safe.

I spoke to my union representative and was told that Principals force the call-in everyday rule all the time and that I wouldn't be helped. I was further told that, as I was the only one affected, it wasn't enough to get the union involved. Basically I was on my own. I went to LMU to see if the Education Department would help me to secure another placement. That was a dead end.

Nope. Still on my own. So, even though I was in danger, I had to return to work. As you can imagine my heart wasn't in it. I still did the best for my students, but was unsure if I wanted to continue teaching. As it turned out, my Principal made that decision for me when she gave me a rotten evaluation and accused me of abandoning my job. Once again I tried to contact my union rep, to no avail. If I thought I was in flames before, this time I fully burnt out and turned to ash. I really wasn't sure of my next step. At that point I did not have a lot of hope.

Hope Rises From the Ashes!

> "Hope rises like a phoenix from the ashes of shattered dreams!" -S.A. Sachs

Because the Principal pettily blacklisted me, I was unable to work for a whole school year. I fell into a deep state of depression. I took the whole year to recuperate mentally and to think about my next move. I wondered if teaching was the right fit for me. It had always been my belief that I would feel different than the way I was feeling then about teaching. Shouldn't it be a little easier if that was what I was meant to do? After all, teaching is a calling, not just a job.

As it turned out, I really loved teaching. So I made peace with my decision and decided to return to teaching even though I knew it probably was not going to be easy; especially since I did not complete my credential program. I was stuck in neutral. I couldn't move forward. So, I did the only thing I could do—I prayed!

The answer to my prayers came in the form of my husband's friend offering me a job in a Catholic school. Since Catholic schools at that time didn't require a credential, I was able to work there. It wasn't easy to go from Special Education to General Education but I felt a change was in order.

Fast forward to the end of the school year and I received communication from LMU that I needed to complete my program, for which I did not have the funds. Once again, I prayed and received the answer from God. Answer to prayer #1, LMU's Dean of Education sat on our board. My principal spoke to and he agreed to pay for my tuition for the year. I was only required to pay some small fees. Answer to prayer #2, in addition to that, the school wanted to pilot a Special Education program, so I was able to pilot an inclusion program and worked with the special needs students at the school for the first semester while I completed school. Won't He do it?!?!

****

Rising from the ashes, I began to shine. I rose from the flames and the ashes through doing what I'm supposed to do. I rose from the flames because I had to. I'm no quitter. I'm a hard worker with a wonderful work ethic.

Me as a mediocre teacher is not something that I'm proud of. However, it is a part of me and I embrace all parts of me; even the worst ME. What I'm most proud of about myself is that I didn't stay there; I did not live in mediocrity.

I am still evolving because I rose from the ashes of my circumstances to become a better version of myself. Like a phoenix, I rise! I know the steps to take. Now, I fight for what I believe in while relying on my faith.

Unlike when I was a struggling as a first year teacher or as a second year teacher who devolved into mediocrity, I now have the knowledge and experience to know what to do. I do not rely on the system as I did all those years ago. If we keep relying on the system, we will stay stuck and not move forward.

My current situation mimics the situation I survived in 2009. Now, I know how to navigate the system and take control. Like a phoenix, I survey the territory. Because of that, I am more equipped to deal with life because being mediocre is not in the card for me; because like a phoenix, I rise!

"Our deepest fear is not that we are inadequate, our deepest fear is that we are powerful beyond measure. It is our light, not our darkness that frightens us. We ask our ourselves – Who am I to be brilliant, gorgeous, talented and fabulous?" – Marianne Williamson

7

by Dr. Kemi Popoola

This poem by Marianne Williamson got me through my most difficult times as a teacher and it reminds me now to simply be brilliant, gorgeous, talented, fabulous, and that I have what it takes to chase after my dreams.

Teaching was supposed to be the thing I did while I was waiting to be admitted into medical school, so needless to say I did not want to become a teacher despite all the people in my life who advised me to become one. I remember vividly the first time I was advised to teach. I was asked to fill in for a teacher who backed out of teaching high school students during the summer of 1994.

At the time, I was a college junior and working in a science lab for the summer. After I was done teaching the class, my then college professor, advisor and boss told me that I was a gifted instructor and I should become a teacher. My response was, "I cannot teach American children…They are too rude and I would not last."

Little did I know that I would come to eat those words years later when I failed to get into medical school. I had just completed a Masters degree in Public Health, and I was once again encouraged to give teaching a try while I waited to get into medical school again. This time, I listened and decided to try teaching. Who knew that I would come to love it!

I remember stepping into my classroom for the first time as an extended substitute teacher and it felt like "home". I discovered that I had a real knack for teaching, especially struggling learners. Maybe it was because of the fact that I did not have such great teachers growing up, or the fact that I was a perfectionist, therefore anything I did I had to give my 100% effort or not at all.

Whatever it was, I found that I not only enjoyed teaching, but learning too because I took my students' successes and failures personal. I loved to see the "light bulb" moments when students got it! I enjoyed watching the growth in my students from the 9th to 12th grade and graduation.

Lesson planning was such a pleasure for me. I scripted my lessons, spent countless hours searching for instructional strategies and authentic assignments for my students. And if my well-choreographed lesson did not go as planned, I assumed the blame. As far as I was concerned, these were "my children" and they mattered.

At the time teaching was all I had going right in my life, so I threw everything I had into it—much to the disappointment of my parents who wanted me to go medical school, get married and have children. Medical school became a distant, ignored and neglected dream that I no longer fed. I threw my entire life into becoming the best teacher I could possibly be.

As the first of seven children, six of whom are girls, my father had always led us to believe that we could be and do anything, but we had to be the best we could be at it. So I decided that if I was going to be a teacher, I had to be the very best teacher. I was a teacher who enjoyed professional development trainings because it meant that I was going to be given tools to be even better.

My students always knew when I had attended a professional development training because that meant that I was going to be sharing and using a new strategy that we had never tried before that very next day. This mindset would later earn me two Teacher of the Month awards and one Teacher of the Year award in my eighth year of teaching. Did I mention that during this time, I met and married the man of my dreams and decided to pursue a Doctoral degree in Curriculum and Instructional Leadership?

I found joy in teaching despite changes in administration, curriculum and teaching assignments. I was there for the students and that was all that mattered to me. So when I was approached by then principal to serve as the 9th grade program coordinator during my sixth year teaching, I did not hesitate, even if it meant extra work without pay and longer hours. I was doing it for my children. That experience would provide the basis for my Doctoral dissertation four years later and open many more doors. I completed the aforementioned dissertation during my eleventh year as a teacher while 6-months pregnant with my son.

****

I think that my disillusion with education began when I was passed over for a position as the freshman instructional coach. They decided to hire someone from another county. That was the first crack in my otherwise "rose-colored glasses" through which I viewed the world, especially the world of teaching. I would be offered the same job a year later, and then fired from that position the following year, which would further widen the crack.

My year out of the classroom as an instructional coach renewed my zest for teaching and renewed my vigor. I plunged myself into improving instruction in the building while simultaneously working on my doctoral program and trying for another baby with my husband.

Then came the summer of 2010, when I was informed that I would not receive a contract since the superintendent decided that schools could no longer purchase instructional coaches with Title I funds—which is financial assistance typically given to schools with high percentages of students from low-income homes.

So I went from a celebrated Teacher of the Year, turned instructional coach to possibly unemployed teacher. That was such a blow to my morale because that was also the same year I had to two miscarriages back-to-back. I was eventually given a teaching contract to return to the classroom, but my joy had diminished. The combination of the two miscarriages and almost getting fired meant that my heart was no longer in the game. I had to begin working my plan B.

****

If it is true that certain people are placed in our lives for a purpose, then in 2011, I would meet the teacher who changed my life forever, Dr. Marquita Blades. Marquita was hired in October of 2011 and we became friends. She was the type of teacher that was super organized and always had fresh ideas, which she did not mind sharing. We traded life stories and teaching strategies and tasks. We were drawn to each other so much so that she introduced me to her then summer work—working with teenagers in the summer as a faculty adviser with the National Youth leadership Forum on Medicine (NYLF).

At the time, I had completed and defended my doctoral dissertation and was now mommy to an adorable baby boy. Marquita encouraged me to step out of my comfort zone and try my hand at being a faculty advisor for the summer in Miami, Florida. Later on that year, she picked up an application for Teacher Support Specialist and encouraged me to apply. Needless to say, that was the foundation for me to, again, pursue positions outside of the classroom. I realized that my reach had exceeded my classroom and it was time for me to make a move.

I applied to positions for a district instructional facilitator first, then as an Assistant Principal within the district, all to no avail. I was receiving rejections after rejections which led me to further question myself and what I knew I capable of doing.

My heart was no longer in teaching daily as it had been in the past 12 years as an educator. I was going through the motions but barely effecting the kind of change that I wanted to see happen in my school. Add to that of going through yet another change in administration, which would be my seventh principal in 12 years.

With the change in administration, I was offered the position of Senior class dean/advisor. The position meant that I would teach part-time (5 classes instead of 6), assume charge of senior discipline, and ultimately track pathway to graduation for 311 senior class students. Of course this also meant many unpaid hours away from my then 14-month-old son and spouse. I was uninterested.

So when I heard that schools would be allowed to once again purchase instructional coaches, I approached my then principal with my resume in hand to request an interview. He turned me down stating that I was not ready as I had not yet "paid my dues". So once again with my crushed spirit, I renewed the search for my next position away from that school and district.

The new position would come through a former colleague that I worked with six years prior. She had moved on to another district and was looking to hire a Graduation Coach for a small alternative school with a population of 300 students. And within the walls of this little alternative school is where I rediscovered my passion for transforming schools and the lives of students through teaching and supporting the teachers.

I was able to see immediate results and what happened when we believe in students and what they are capable of achieving. I saw the impact of providing wraparound support such as mental and medical health, in addition to providing a great education. Listening to students who would otherwise not have achieved a high school diploma due to academic mistakes in their past, and watching them walk across the stage to receive their diplomas was the greatest feeling in the world.

I was later promoted from Graduation Coach to School Improvement Coordinator, which meant that I was now seated at the table to add my voice and expertise to transforming a school from a low-performing and failing school to a successful one. At this school the learning was just as important as teaching. It was no longer enough that teachers taught the standards, student learning was placed in the fore-front of all decisions by the administration.

As a School Improvement Coordinator I was able to co-write and receive an additional $1 million in funds that would allow this school to sustain these supports over time. The newly funded school-based health clinic allowed students to access healthcare services during the day while at school, and help reduce barriers to access of care such as cost, transportation, and inconvenience.

There was so much that I enjoyed about my new district, most important was the fact that my contribution as an educator was not only sought by other educators, but was recognized as well. My current position as a high school administrator is the culmination of all my life's experiences and hard work.

I am able to draw upon teaching, coaching and administrative experiences to support the transformation of my new school in the position of an Assistant Principal, and I cannot be any happier. This position, with its many daily challenges, has also given me a renewed sense of hope and encouragement. It has proven to me once and for all that there are no wasted experiences. All experiences are necessary in your life journey towards discovering your niche in life.

~The End~

ABOUT THE AUTHOR

Dr. Marquita S. Blades is an award-winning Educator, international speaker, author, and education consultant with 16 years of experience as a high school science teacher and manager of national Science, Technology, Engineering and Math (STEM) programs for high-achieving high school students. During her time working with public school districts, she also served as a curriculum & assessment developer and professional learning facilitator for multiple school districts in the metropolitan Atlanta area.

Dr. Blades is currently a full-time Education Consultant, the owner of Dr. Blades Consulting, and the host of The Dr. Marquita Blades Show-Candid

Conversations that Create Change, a radio show dedicated to discussing current trends and issues in education. Dr. Blades' Consulting firm offers solutions to learning institutions and individuals through professional development programs, curriculum and assessment development, and conference development and programming services. Dr. Blades is also the founder of The Mediocre Teacher Project© which helps other teachers avoid and battle through burnout by incorporating their unique gifts and talents into their daily practice. Dr. Blades has presented at numerous conferences including the International Academic Forum, International Conference on Innovation in Science Education, and the Innovative Schools Summit.

Dr. Blades earned a Bachelor of Interdisciplinary Studies in Broad Field Science from Georgia State University, a Master of Science in Technical and Professional Communication from Southern Polytechnic State University, and a Doctor of Education in Instructional Leadership from Nova Southeastern University. When she is not working, Dr. Blades enjoys reading, cooking, and traveling with her husband.

For more information, you can visit Dr. Blades' website: www.drmarquitablades.com

Follow her on Social Media:
Facebook: Dr. Blades Consulting
Twitter: @DrMBlades
LinkedIn: Dr. Marquita Smith Blades

FOOTNOTES

[1]. American Federation of Teachers. (2017, November 03). 2017 Educator Quality of Life Survey. Retrieved from https://www.aft.org/2017-educator-quality-life-survey

[2]. America's Future: The Inside Story. (2012, January 14). Teachers Committing Suicide: When Will the Bashing Stop? Retrieved from http://americasfutureinsidestory.blogspot.com/2012/01/teachers-committing-suicide-when-will.html

[3]. Wood, H. (2013). 6 Lessons I Learned as a Student Teacher. Schools of Thought CNN. Retrieved from http://schoolsofthought.blogs.cnn.com/2013/06/17/from-career-to-classroom-6-things-i-learned-as-a-student-teacher/

[4]. Pierson, R. (2013). Every kid needs a champion. TED Talks. Retrieved from https://www.ted.com/talks/rita_pierson_every_kid_needs_a_champion

www.ingramcontent.com/pod-product-compliance
Lightning Source LLC
Chambersburg PA
CBHW032127090426
42743CB00007B/501